TEXT

TEXT

"Me? I don't read books!" Irnerio says.

"What do you read, then?"

"Nothing. I've become so accustomed to not reading that I don't even read what appears before my eyes. It's not easy: they teach us to read as children, and for the rest of our lives we remain the slaves of all the written stuff they fling in front of us. I may have had to make some effort myself, at first, to learn not to read, but now it comes quite naturally to me. The secret is not refusing to look at the written words. On the contrary, you must look at them, intensely, until they disappear." –

from *'If in a Winter's Night a traveller'* – *Italo Calvino*

CONVENTIONAL LANGUAGE IS ABOUT ITS SUBJECT

conventional? What did Ian Hamilton Finlay mean by conventional? Veronica Forrest-Thomson, (how different poetry would have been if you had not been killed in 1974) wrote:

"It is easy to treat poetry as if it were engaged in the language-game of giving information and thus to assume that what is important about a poem is what it tells us about the external world. The meaning of the poem is extended into the world...Such an approach falsifies our experience of poems, reduces the distinctiveness of poetry, and neglects many of the components of poetic language, but it is an intellectually less taxing approach which triumphs for that reason..."

The reference to a language-game coming, of course, from the influential philosopher of language Ludwig Wittgenstein:

"Poetry is a language-game not primarily concerned with the transmission of information". Wittgenstein identified the totality of propositions as language. Language is the sum set of all subaltern sets operating across landscapes in which descriptive facility and functionality is synonymous with their fabric – the *fabric of the (language) act synonymous with its content*. Synonymous but not the same.

Charles Bernstein writes: "Content never equals meaning". How does this square with the view that poetic (or scientific) language is different from conventional language – if conventional language is about its content, but any language act is synonymous. American poet Lynn Hejinian answers: reality remains identical to itself in
form
but not sum

       AND WITH THE UBIQUITY OF (COMMERCIAL) TYPOGRAPHY,

        in every moment of your waking life you can see a text – this page. Look up from this page – in any glance in any direction you will see another text. You are immersed in text. You describe your experience to yourself in language and every aspect of your visual field is labelled, text-overlaid

THE OMNIPRESENCE OF A PLENARY UNIFORMIST LANGUAGE IN THE PUBLIC

       and through a hierarchy of mediations, the private

       DOMAIN HAS ENMESHED THE TEXT INTO THE "EFFICIENT" AND "TRANSPARENT" – PRINCIPLES OF GRAPHIC DESIGN/LANGUAGE commercial design has absorbed the craft and inspiration of modernist graphic innovations, while

UNIFIED AS THE VISUAL HEGEMONY OF PACKAGING, IDENTITY AND COMMODITY.

"Thus how do we read what is meant *precisely* to be read? That is given for no other purpose, and without distraction (even those distractions which we often take as the stigmata of "reading" but are really those of entertainment, those of good fog)", wrote Bruce Andrews.

To Veronica Forrest-Thomson's observation that there would be no point in writing poetry unless poetry were different from everyday language, it should be added that poetry similarly has no point if it is the same as advertising language.

THE AURAL DEBRIS OF FURNITURE MUSIC BURYING CONSCIOUSNESS IN ORGANISED MARKETING NOISE IS THE SHARED

(unacknowledged)

FATE FOR TEXT.

In 1916 Eric Satie performed his work 'musique d'ameublement', literally furniture music; music heard but not listened to. It was the first ever *muzak*; Satie foreseeing the time when our lives would be filled with unheeded music. While ignoring this contemporary sound track most of the time, we are conscious that it is there, neutered, affecting our moods, altering our behaviour. This musical accompaniment is a new phenomenon – less than one hundred years old; in a same period of time, text

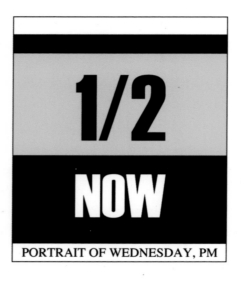

1/2

NOW

PORTRAIT OF WEDNESDAY, PM

one day split open – Philip Davenport

has become furniture text, text seen but not read – logos, signs, advertisements, labels – affecting our moods, altering our behaviour, constructing our experience of reality, changing our attitudes in an assumption of universal literacy and 'the fallacy of unmediated expression'.

RESTRICTING THE DEFINITION OF LITERACY

Bruce Andrews: "Objective assumptions, which ground meaning in reference to the world outside and which relate self-evidence of objects to the practical task of learning to read, provide only one scenario" – what Charles Bernstein calls the tyranny of the familiar – a manufactured consensus of models of competence "a coercive organisation of grammar, rhetoric, technical format, & ideological symbols": "It is the terrorist function of forms (and of institutions deriving from these forms) to maintain the illusions of transparency and reality and to disguise the forms that maintain reality." – Henri Lefebvre

Literacy is

a social construction and is significant in determining, and being determined by, the prevailing social order.

Literacy is

a relative construct and is in practice context dependent. Global definitions therefore are both elusive and unattainable

TO CONSENSUALISED STANDARD PUBLIC ORGANISATION, LANGUAGE IS CO-OPTED TO APPROVED CENTRAL MEANINGS

"Everything in our age conspires to turn the writer, and every other kind of artist as well, into a minor official, working on

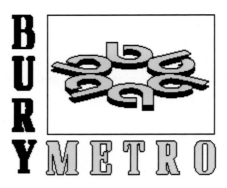

*Every item of promotional or informative nature must
carry the corporate logo in the prescribed manner*

themes handed down from above and never telling what seems to him the whole of the truth" noted George Orwell in The Prevention of Literature or as Guy Debord observed it as the "sprint between independent artists and the police to test and develop the use of new techniques of conditioning" or after 20 years of national arts policy, the arts are mobilised to:

1. Develop a Stronger Community Spirit;

2. Improve Transport and the Environment;

3. Create a Better Future for All generations;

4. Make our communities Safer and Healthier;

5. Achieve Social Inclusion;

6. Develop a Competitive and Diverse Local Economy;

Hence the need for the Official Verse Culture

AND DECANTED THROUGH A HIERARCHY OF MEDIATIONS TO ALLOW ONLY POETRY EXPRESSIONS OF EXEMPLARY PERSONAL NARRATIVES.

the (pre)dominant "poetic" factor of poetry is embedded in self-reflexivity, the first person, the voice of the poet, sharing an epiphanous moment, his or her narrow emotional life or simply a wry anecdote. As the British rhyme-writer Sophie Hannah would have it: the best thing about being a poet is "being able to get a relatively civilised revenge on anyone who treats you really nastily – and plenty of people do! – by writing something cutting about them"...

... an intellectually less taxing approach which triumphs for that reason...

"The production of ignorance that is enforced by restraints on complexity of thought; political, social, and aesthetic content; and form" according to Charles Bernstein.

In this Official Verse Culture, "The world is found to be meaningful, but not for and to itself; it is meaningful because perceiving it makes the poet special; the poet plunders the world for its perceptual, spiritual treasure and becomes worthy (and worth more) on that basis" – Lynn Hejinian.

It will be as if Modernism never happened, this representational/narrative art (with its concomitant fallacy of unmediated expression) with patron saints celebrated for their advertisement rhymes as much for their lyricism.

O, *the Lyric*

held as axiomatic, itself a vocal heritage of language drawn from poetry's archaic roots as the story-telling accompaniment to rhythmic tunes, pre-modern and therefore strictly tonal.

Despite Robert Grenier's seminal 1971 declaration I HATE SPEECH;

Despite even Adorno's question of the implication in the Holocaust, the British Lyric Tradition, its margins of landscape and voice, renews itself in dismal paddling further into its backwater to privilege dialect and regionalism – 'authentic' Northern voices (or more recently rural southern voices) instead of the dynamic experimental uncertainty of Bob Cobbing and the Writer's Forum or the need to animate a millennial Modernism in dialogue with international Concrete Poetry, LANGUAGE or OULIPO,

but it is an intellectually less taxing approach which triumphs for that reason...

from 'Bob Jubile' - Bob Cobbing

The practice of text art in public space stems from conceptual art's critique of the materiality and economics of the art object, a fusion of the work with its site and context of display, and liberation of possibilities for unmediated public distribution. This liberating dialogue between the reader and writer, a continually evolving context of process and actuality, has been denied by the backwater cultural constriction of the poet to the page, the reading, or the advertisement copy. Meanwhile Culture driven by massive global forces, History re-started, Science and the Image move on. The marginal language of song? Poetry? It's irrelevant. "Me? I don't read". Let them sell *their* Past of anthologies for Christmas, birthdays, funerals, and the next war ...

THE QUESTION OF FORM IS OUR ONLY CONSTANT CONNECTION WITH THE PAST. ALTHOUGH THE GREAT FORMS OF THE PAST WERE THE SONNET

The history of poetry over-written with all the drama and import of a nursery rhyme forgets in the fourth century A.D., Optatianus Porfyrius published a permutational poem called Carmen XXV. With words fixed in its fifth column, words in other columns can be arbitrarily shuffled with each other, creating a fixed form poem with words shuffling to 1.62 billion possible permutations of the text.

By the Renaissance (1561), Julius Caesar Scaliger was able to establish word permutation poems (Proteus Verse) as one of the canonical poetical forms of the 17th Century.

Trace the real Past from there to here.

On to 1961: the French writer Raymond Queneau, published 'Cent Mille Milliards de Poèmes', which is constructed of ten basic sonnets, sliced into 14 strips, one per line of sonnet text. By flipping the strips to left or right, the reader obtains a combination of lines making up a sonnet. Every one of the possible sonnets is structurally perfect and makes perfect sense but the incremental arithmetic is such that it would not be possible to read all the possible variations in one life-time.

(As William Carlos Williams wrote: "*All* sonnets mean the same thing")

OR FREE VERSE,

In contemporary verse, how many 'poems' can stand the prose test of removal of their arbitrary line breaks or the mock portentous hush of the poet's reading?

"Should humanity lie back and be satisfied to watch new thoughts make ancient verses? We don't believe that it should." – Francois Le Lionnais

The key modernist project is the question of the nature of the medium. This is the terrain that the 2005 Text Festival in Bury seeks to examine: what are the innovations and devices that characterise the tradition of poetic innovation and what is their relationship to contemporary visual text art practice? "Valorizing form has its limits", there is a danger in focusing on the means at the expense of the meaning, a catalogue of devices and methodologies, but in engaging with the debate about the future of text and poetry it should be productive to examine the tools currently available.

And so what if it's not? Remember you don't read poetry.

TEXT, THE FUTURE

"To construct room for further efforts" – Bob Perelman,

WILL DIALECTICALLY RISE FROM A GLASS BEAD GAME OF

"a way of *reconstituting* language by unpacking the toolbox" applying to performative writing sound, text, digital, environmental and performance.

PARATAXIS,

is simply the juxtaposition of two elements or clauses without a conjunction. One sentence is placed next to another which has no obvious relevance. This practice is most familiar in the Haiku tradition which frequently uses the enigmatic effect to generate the deeper meaning in a poem. Making the sentence the basic unit of composition as opposed to traditional Western poetry's focus on the line, poets and artists using text, thus require the reader's participation in the sense-making process.

The paratactic tension achieved in poetry is mirrored in contemporary text art practice which frequently juxtaposes a sentence unit as *paratactic* to its location; the meaning of a text located in a public space resonates in the collage of the words with their location. Lawrence Weiner's WATER MADE IT WET had toured mainly gallery based locations until finding its home on the Cricket Path Bridge in Radcliffe; the economic accuracy of its textual intervention creates a paratactic dialogue unifying the experience of the bridge in the landscape "the decision as to condition rests with the receiver upon the occasion of receivership."

The New Sentence (coined by Ron Silliman) is significant because its formal properties place it at the centre of a number of non-narrative techniques driving a political as

WATER MADE IT WET – Lawrence Weiner

well as poetic challenge to the accepted structures in contemporary poetry. In paratactic writing the autonomous meaning of a sentence is heightened, questioned, and changed by the degree of separation or connection that the reader perceives with regard to the surrounding sentences.

INTERTEXTUALITY,

more recently the curatorial theorist Nicolas Bourriaud coining the phrase 'postproduction' from TV film and music editing/recording/channel-flicking for the ever increasing practice of creating artworks (of all types) from pre-existing works, artists and writers interpreting, reproducing, appropriating cultural products into new works.

Intertextuality posits that a text does not exist as a self-sufficient whole, hermetically sealed. The writer is a reader of texts before s/he is a creator of texts, and therefore the act of writing – text or poem – is inevitably shot through with references, quotations and influences of every kind. Moreover the reader reads the text immersed in texts. A text is available only through some process of reading; what is produced at the moment of reading is due to the cross-fertilisation of the packaged textual material by all the texts which the reader brings to it. Readers embody texts. The reader is surrounded by texts, advertising, signs, exits, numbers on doors, names on shirts, your watch, every where you look, every text you read is intermingled with the text world in which you are embedded. Texts are reading you. Quotation containing quotations embedded in quotations – It's staring you in the face.

Carolyn Thompson's recent work explores this relationship between text creator and text with works that generate a new text from an 'original' other, drawing on an implicit subtext or

After Easton Ellis – Carolyn Thompson

principle supplying the constructive rule. "After Easton Ellis" consists of 384 sheets of paper cut to the size of the leaves of the Picador publication of *American Psycho*. Consumerism is a dominant theme in the novel, so Thompson's appropriation reduces the original to a new work leaving only the hundreds of brand names in their original arrangement. Similarly, in "Winston and Julia: A Love Story", Thompson eliminates much of the original text from George Orwell's *Nineteen Eighty-Four* leaving only the passages featuring the love of Winston and Julia and thus creates a new intense textual work of operatic passion.

MATERIALITY,

text as a material, has a long history that can be traced back to ideogrammatic languages of ancient civilisations. Futurism, Dada, Surrealism, Constructivism and Cubism all made use of text materially. Since the Sixties, the principal manifestations of text as material build on the discoveries of Concrete Poetry (the first truly international poetry movement) and Conceptual Art. Although intended to be critical, Veronica Forrest-Thomson's observation that Concrete Poetry carried discontinuity with ordinary language to its limits by seeking a point where language ceases to be language and becomes simply material, visual or aural, for making patterns is accurate, only missing Eugen Gomringer's conclusion that: "The purpose of reduced language is not the reduction of language itself but the achievement of greater flexibility and freedom of communication (with its inherent need for rules and regulations)."

Since Marcel Duchamp's invention of the 'ready-made' in 1909, Conceptual Art has developed approaches involving installation, ready-mades, documentation and words "where the concept, proposition or investigation is presented in the form of language". Sol LeWitt, wrote in his *Sentences on Conceptual Art* (1969) "Ideas can be works of art; they are in a chain of development that may eventually find some form. All ideas need not be made physical." One of the leading figures of late 20th Century art, Lawrence Weiner famously wrote:

(1) THE ARTIST MAY CONSTRUCT THE PIECE.
(2) THE PIECE MAY BE FABRICATED.
(3) THE PIECE NEED NOT BE BUILT.

> Each being equal and consistent with the intent of the artist, the decision as to condition rests with the receiver upon the occasion of receivership.

Despite 40 years of conceptual art practice, the material of language as a visual arts medium continues to challenge traditional notions of art as object, narrative or representation. It is a challenge that the poetry mainstream continues to fail to meet.

"Reading as a particular reading, an enactment, a co-production" (Bruce Andrews) may best be applied to Hester Reeve's remarkable work *Being and Time*. The artist adopts reading, writing and thinking and re-presentation of them as modes of 'Being.' Reeve sitting at a desk for nine weeks, reading and transcribing by hand Heidegger's *Being and Time*, presenting the work of art as a 'passport to a conceptual kingdom,' as an embodied processual effort as well as a concrete/material object to be viewed in the gallery.

SPATIALISATION,

relates closely to the use of language as a material, foregrounding the transition of the language object into (actual or virtual) three-dimensions; described by Charles Bernstein as words freed of the tyranny of horizontality. Max Bense observed: "the three-dimensional language object is the carrier of a specifically concrete aesthetic message." The spatialisation of a text generates a tension between the particular of the text mark/act and the generality of its space, organised spatially, highlighting non-linguistic ground, breaking down the meaning-bearing elements of language into graphic signs.

The spatialisation of language is a frequent operation in text art installation, with words fracturing across a location. "There is no such thing as an empty space or an empty time. There is always something to see, something to hear" – John Cage.

Word-text-spaces, actually, virtually or metaphorically, spatialised can be conjugated in such a way that their *positions* imply 'verbs' in the spaces (silences) between them. This invisible grammar can be read within and between categories. The linguistics of interval, position and duration are usually closed off by line rules and structures and dimensional limits, but "placement as a grammatical concept can be extended to any abstraction... to a degree we may speak of meaning as a system of permutations, as a mathematics of placement..." – Sigmund Bode.

To read/hear a spatialised text constitutes a test for the reader, constructing readings based on the order that the senses collide with the words, offering alternate readings, multiple readings, generating meanings from the vocabulary of placement. Place and Time and Duration – qualities of poetry. The modern scientific understanding of the non-

'High Fidelity' (2004) — Hester Reeve (the HRH)

linearity of space and time is mirrored in text-in-space/time experimentation and its the most familiar form of spatialisation in digital text and film animation.

RESTRICTED LANGUAGES

> First glyph; then syllabary,
> Then letters.
> *Louis Zukofsky – 'A'*

Language operates with rules (of grammar, syntax, spelling); poetry adds further rules such as counting syllables, rhythmic beats, or lines. A constraint is an axiom of a text and invented poetic rules become central to poetic cultures. Shakespeare working within the rigid constraints of the sonnet nevertheless produced some of the most original, inspired, and long-appreciated poetry known to the world. As Queneau points out "the poet has always been dependent at least on elementary arithmetic. If he wants to write an alexandrine he must be able to count up to 12; for a sonnet, up to fourteen, and for a sonnet in alexandrines up to 168". The arbitrariness of one form over another – the established culture's endorsement – has over the last fifty years been directly challenged for ethical, political and artistic reasons. The artistic avant-gardes of the 20th century reinvented poetic forms on occasion assuming the notion of arbitrariness adopting a poetics of indeterminacy and chance. Tristan Tzara created Dada poetry by cutting out the words of a newspaper article, shuffling them in a bag and writing them down in the accidental order they had been pulled out. Despite the anti-art gesture, Tzara's strategy to select, break up and permute a group of words can be traced back to the 16th Century and

Roughly 92% Angel but about 8% Devil – Edward Ruscha

Julius Caesar Scaliger. All pre-20th century permutation poems shuffle a fixed set of data directly inscribed into them. However, moving on from Tzara's innovation, in the sixties, John Cage and Jackson Mac Low engaged directly with the arbitrary, generating a number of poetic (and musical) works with process/random decisions related to source text selection and ordering using I Ching chance operations.

The most systematic and determined exploration of new poetic rule forms has been the primarily French phenomenon OULIPO (the Ouvroir de litterature potentielle – the Workshop of Potential Literature). The already mentioned "sonnet machine" of Queneau is perhaps the best known work of an enigmatic OULIPO Workshop he founded in 1960 with mathematician – Francois de Lionnais. Aside from the element of creative fun went a sincere interest in exploring implications and possibilities for new language processing literature. What happens to language under the constraints of structural formulae and how far can it be driven before reaching limits of intelligibility? This might sound similar to Surrealist, Concrete and particularly Dadaist ideas, but while Dada aimed to break down the rules, OULIPO's focus was in creating new ones – famously proclaimed: 'A text written according to a constraint describes the constraint.' It generated numerous new (often deliberately simple) forms rather than necessarily new literature, such as S+7 which consists in taking a text and replacing each substantive with the seventh following it in a dictionary (N+7 replaces the nouns) or the lipogram (a rediscovery from as early as the Sixth Century) in which the writer excludes one or several letters of the alphabet. The most famous example is the novel *La Disparation* by George Perec in which there are no 'e's. More recently in what might be called a

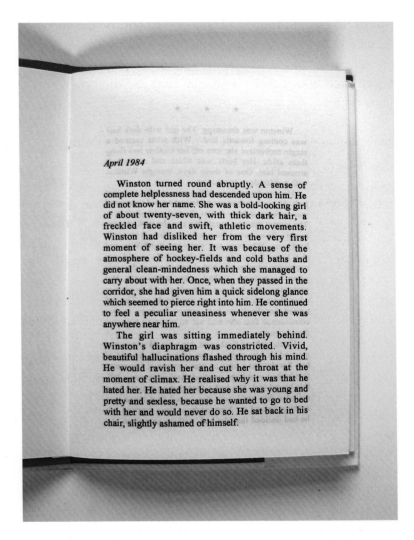

April 1984

Winston turned round abruptly. A sense of complete helplessness had descended upon him. He did not know her name. She was a bold-looking girl of about twenty-seven, with thick dark hair, a freckled face and swift, athletic movements. Winston had disliked her from the very first moment of seeing her. It was because of the atmosphere of hockey-fields and cold baths and general clean-mindedness which she managed to carry about with her. Once, when they passed in the corridor, she had given him a quick sidelong glance which seemed to pierce right into him. He continued to feel a peculiar uneasiness whenever she was anywhere near him.

The girl was sitting immediately behind. Winston's diaphragm was constricted. Vivid, beautiful hallucinations flashed through his mind. He would ravish her and cut her throat at the moment of climax. He realised why it was that he hated her. He hated her because she was young and pretty and sexless, because he wanted to go to bed with her and would never do so. He sat back in his chair, slightly ashamed of himself.

Winston & Julia: A Love Story – Carolyn Thompson

post-OULIPO development the Canadian poet, Christian Bök's book *Eunoia* is made up of 5 chapters each one limited to words containing each vowel in turn.

Critically, how does a poem (paratactic, intertextual, material, spatial or constrained) answer the charge that it is simply a package of language games, no more poetic than a puzzle, or even plain nonsense? Charles Bernstein's defence of poetry challenges the claim that the officially-approved use of language is *actually* 'transparent':

> Indeed you say that
> nonsenese shed leds on its "antithesis"
> sense-making: but teally the antithsisi
> of these poems you call nonselnse is not
> sense-making itslef but perhps, in some
> cases, the simulation of sense-making:
> decitfullness, manifulation, the
> media-ization of language, etc.

The poetic function is manifested when an utterance is ordered additionally in a way which cannot be justified by the usual requirements of linguistic communication. Each being equal and consistent with the intent of the artist, the decision as to condition rests with the receiver upon the occasion of receivership. Lynn Hejinian has identified the gradation or duration of enlightenment to increased insight, what she has called 'delayed coherence'. The answer to Simon Armitage's question "Is the effort to decode them greater than the final reward?"

is yes.

With Wittgenstein's assertion that language itself is a game, the privileging of an 'accepted form' (an intellectually less taxing approach which triumphs for that reason) over the struggle for meaning through language is exposed as value-driven and ideologically based.

IN THE FACE OF THE PARADOX OF LANGUAGE'S MILITARISATION

"War, it will be seen, accomplishes the necessary destruction, but accomplishes it in a psychologically acceptable way. In principle it would be quite simple to waste the surplus labour of the world by building temples and pyramids, by digging holes and filling them up again, or even by producing vast quantities of goods and then setting fire to them. But this would provide only the economic and not the emotional basis for a hierarchical society. What is concerned here is not the morale of masses, whose attitude is unimportant so long as they are kept steadily at work," said George Orwell.

One leading spokesman for the Project for the American Century, former CIA Director James Woolsey, unabashedly declared in 2004 "we are already fighting World War III." The reconstruction contracts have been granted. To the Empire of Freedom you are either with us or you are against us.

Perhaps not what Beckett was thinking when he wrote "Let us hope the time will come, thank God that in certain circles it has already come, when language is most efficiently used where it is being most efficiently misused" in the war on abstract nouns.

"Instead of making art I filled out this form" (using the sentence as the unit of composition).

AND DE-MILITARISATION,

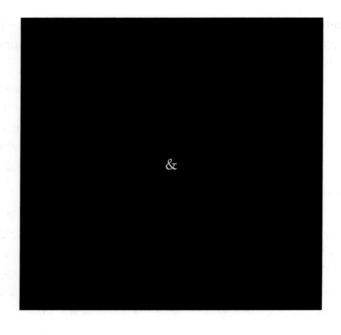

Ampersand – Caroline Bergvall

"Poetry must involve more than the filling out of forms – the exercise of formalities; it requires an invention of form."
– Lynn Hejinian

Syntax, like government, can only be obeyed.
It is therefore of no use except when you
have something particular to command
such as: Go buy me a bunch of carrots.
– John Cage

INVENTION OF NEW LANGUAGE FORMS,

Maurice Merleau-Ponty wrote: everything signifies everything; concatenate this with Wittgenstein's "The word 'is' figures as the copula, as a sign for identity, and as an expression for existence; we speak of something, but also of something's happening. (In the proposition, 'Green is green'--where the first word is the proper name of a person and the last an adjective--these words do not merely have different meanings: they are different symbols.)" and Donald Rumsfeld can add the comment that the five groups opposing U.S. forces in Iraq – identified as looters, criminals, remnants of Saddam Hussein's government, foreign terrorists and Iranian-backed Shiites – "are all slightly different in why they are there and what they are doing... That doesn't make it anything like a guerrilla war or an organized resistance. It makes it like five different things going on in which the groups are functioning more like terrorists." A reporter quoted the Pentagon's own definition of guerrilla war – "military and paramilitary operations conducted in enemy-held or hostile territory by irregular ground indigenous forces" – and told Rumsfeld that it "Seems to fit a lot of what's going on in Iraq."

To which Rumsfeld replied: "It really doesn't."

All norms of other kinds of discourse are changed when absorbed by a poem, and that syntax in conjunction with convention is the agent of this change:

measure the degree of disorder in their system
it is a matter of common experience
disorder will tend to increase if things are left to themselves
Order can create order out of disorder but cleaves
expenditure
effort or energy
so decreases the amount of order
Woe for our unhappy town!
Woe for thee, O lands that nurse thy little babes!

LANGUAGE

AS A MATERIAL AND FIELD OF ENQUIRY

"Poetry must involve more than the filling out of forms – the exercise of formalities; it requires an *invention of form*." Lynn Hejinian.

MUST BE THE RESPONSE TO THE CHALLENGE OF CHANGING EXPERIENCE.

Paratactic, intertextual, material, spatialised, and process-rule-constricted

INNOVATION IS THE NEGATION OF THE GIVEN –

The absence of this negation, the hegemony of the given, is the real reason for the lack of public interest in poetry – it's not the marketing but the product that is at fault.

THE CONTINUITY OF DISCOVERY BEYOND THE COLONIZED

"a kind of reservation for good savages who (without realizing

nondescript — Shaun Pickard

In The Graveyard – Hester Reeve (the HRH)

it) make modern society, with the rapid increase in its technological powers and the forced expansion of its market, work" Guy Debord.

AND THE FUTURE OF TEXTUALITY

The failure of poetry will be the failure of poets to challenge Poetry and the forces which would have it fail. The way forward is not thru the basement door as Bruce Andrews observed, but in the direct challenge to the dead weight of British (and American) poetic conservativism,

WILL REST NOT WITH THE GATEKEEPERS, controlling access and distribution, academic and social discourse, ("education teach us to read as children, and for the rest of our lives we remain the slaves of all the written stuff they fling in front of us"), a curriculum that teaches poetry's irrelevance, that language can only be used in approved and prize-winning ways, "to divert the taste for the new, which has in our era become a threat to it, into certain debased forms of novelty, which are entirely harmless and muddled" – Guy Debord

BUT AS IT ALWAYS HAS,

despite the history of appropriation and forgetting, a consistently powerful counter-hegemonic stream has historically played a central role in most of the Art Movements of the twentieth century set out to reinvent and challenge the language of expression. Futurism, Dada, Surrealism, Fluxus, Conceptualism, were all, first and foremost, literary/language movements and as Ron Silliman has persuasively demonstrated, historically it is the banality of the Establishment poets that fades into obscurity. The future of textual work will in the future be as ignored as every other previous future has until it is the past

WITH THE RESTLESS, THE INVESTIGATORS OF LANGUAGE,

Ron Silliman writes: "all practitioners of post-avant writing have had to confront such questions of form, content, coherency, implication, context, responsibility and any other number of qualities of the poem from scratch. On average, they have had to work much harder and far more thoughtfully than their counterparts on the far side of the genre in almost anything they have written. & when they don't do their homework, it shows immediately. There may be self-delusion, but there is no hiding allowed for post-avant poets."

crowd horror at the gait of a mistake
      there are local degrees of freedom
      classes of excitations
      to believe the heroes' recipe.

"In a passionate age, the crowd would cheer his courage and tremble
as he tried to reach it. But in an age without passion,
people would agree that it was unreasonable to venture out so far,
      and think each other clever
      for figuring this out.

~~admire~~ ourselves.
The possibility of 'fresh' perception, the ability of the TEXT to outflank perception and make the receiver experience the object in question as if for the first time. The recipe for

the New itself then cannot be new, "The concept of defamiliarisation was not invented by the Russian Formalists; Romantic writers from Goethe and Wordsworth to Proust had discussed the power of particular linguistic forms to create 'strangeness'" (Marjorie Perloff); Ezra Pound's call for poets to "Make it new" is still the imperative.

WHO DISCLOSE AND CONSTRUCT EXPERIENCE

the non-linearity of much so-called disjunctive poetry comma itself a point of contact with everyday experiences; Text must be made by all – but text defined as enquiry, as seeking new understandings in how language works, how reality is constructed, how life is lived, and changed

AND MEANINGS

"The language of poetry is a language of inquiry, not the language of a genre. It is that language in which a writer (or a reader) both perceives and is conscious of the perception. Poetry, therefore, takes as its premise that language is a medium for experiencing experience."

IN THE SUBSTANTIAL

AMBIGUITY OF LANGUAGE

Conventional language is about its subject and with the ubiquity of (commercial) typography, the omnipresence of a plenary uniformist language in the public domain has enmeshed the text into the "efficient" and "transparent" – principles of graphic design/language unified as the visual hegemony of packaging, identity and commodity.

The aural debris of furniture music burying consciousness in organised marketing noise is the shared fate for text. Restricting the definition of literacy to consensualised standard public organisation, language is co-opted to approved central meanings and decanted through a hierarchy of mediations to allow only poetry expressions of exemplary personal narratives.

The question of form is our only constant connection with the past. Although the great forms of the past were the sonnet or free verse. Text the future will dialectically rise from a glass bead game of
Parataxis,
Intertextuality, Materiality,
Spatialisation, Restricted Languages

Faced with the paradox of language's militarisation and de-militarisation, invention of new language forms, new literacies, language as a material and field of enquiry must be the response to the challenge of changing experience. Innovation is the negation of the given – the continuity of discovery beyond the colonized sector and the future of text, will rest not with the gatekeepers, but as it always has, with the restless, the investigators of language who disclose and construct experience and meanings in the substantial ambiguity of language

Colophon

Text

Published 2005
Edition of 1000

Bury Metropolitan Borough Council
Athenaeum House
Market St
Bury
BL9 0BP
UNITED KINGDOM

Tel: 0161 253 5869
Fax: 0161 253 5915

ISBN 0-9538915-3-4

Designed by Alan Ward @
www.axisgraphicdesign.co.uk
Printed by Editoriale Bortolazzi Stei,
Verona, Italy
Fonts: The Sans and The Mix, Lucas Fonts, Berlin
Materials: text printed on Artic Volume 150gsm,
endpapers printed on Freelife Merida Fedrigoni
140gsm, flexibound in Laminel

Endpapers:
"Weave" – Things Not Worth Keeping (cris cheek
& Kirsten Lavers)